TONI CARMINE SALERNO

GODDESS

The Eternal Feminine

WITHIN LIFE AND NATURE

BLUE ANGEL®
PUBLISHING

Goddess:
The Eternal Feminine
Within Life and Nature

Second edition
Copyright © 2013 Toni Carmine Salerno
First edition published in 2006

Published by
Blue Angel Publishing®
80 Glen Tower Drive, Glen Waverley,
Victoria, Australia 3150

E-mail: info@blueangelonline.com
Website: www.blueangelonline.com

Written and illustrated by Toni Carmine Salerno
Edited by Tanya Graham

Blue Angel is a registered trademark of Blue Angel Gallery Pty. Ltd.

ISBN: 978-1-922161-04-8

Preface

THE PAINTINGS AND WRITINGS IN THIS BOOK
were inspired by the sacred energy of the eternal Goddess – her energy
exists not just in every woman but also in nature and in the stars above
us – she touches the hearts of everyone and all of life upon this planet.

The Goddess is an infinite pool of creativity. It is her spirit that flows
through my work. Her love and wisdom guides and inspires me.
The eternal feminine is my greatest source of inspiration, both in my
life and work.

I'm often asked why I paint mainly women. The answer is; I love
portraying the beauty of the feminine form, whether it be the feminine
forms of trees, nature, the moon, the ocean or women. It is my way
of honouring the Goddess throughout creation. Plus, the world can
do with a little more feminine energy, a bit more softening, a bit more
nurturing, beauty and compassion. This planet has been dominated
by men for far too long and the balance needs to be restored. Positive
change is occurring, albeit very slowly in some parts of the world. The
Goddess is re-emerging and we can all benefit from her wisdom, love,
beauty and creativity, qualities that all women possess.

I hope that something in this book inspires you, I hope something
in this book helps you in some way. As you travel along your life's
journey, I encourage you to pursue your dream. Believe in yourself,
believe in the dream and don't give up until the dream in your heart
manifests in your reality.

This book may also be used as an oracle. To do this, simply place
your hand on the front cover of the book and close your eyes.
Gently bring your focus within as you observe your breath. Just be
aware of yourself being breathed in by the Universe. As you breathe in,
imagine breathing in the healing and guiding light of the Goddess.
As you breathe out, breathe out any concern, fear or anxiety. Feel these
negative emotions and thoughts dissolving into light as you release

them with each breath out. Let go of past, present or future concerns and just be fully present within each moment. Breathe in light – breathe out love.

Once you feel calm and centered, focus on something that is currently troubling you or that you would like clarification on. Ask any question that relates to this situation or problem. Then open the book randomly and read the first thing that you are drawn to. Take your time. Feel the words; allow them into your heart and above all, keep an open mind. Observe the image next to the message, again taking your time and allow the vibrations of the image to flow into you. As it is often said, a picture speaks a thousand words.

The words and images in this book are ultimately vibrations – beyond them exists an underlying healing energy. In the silence and stillness of your heart exists the greatest truth and the most profound peace is found in the empty space between your thoughts.

With eternal love,
Toni Carmine Salerno

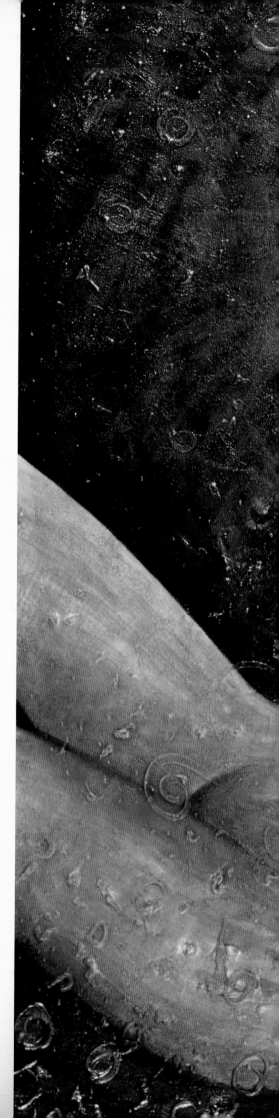

I COME TO
YOU IN YOUR
DREAMS.
I AM
hope
- DESIRE -

ALL WITHIN
YOU
THAT YEARNS
TO BE

YOUR TRUE ESSENCE

EXISTS ETERNALLY IN A *world of light*

YOU ARE THE ESSENCE OF CREATION

ALL THAT YOU IMAGINE LOVINGLY YOU CREATE

LOVE = CREATION

LOVE IS ALL THERE IS

The real you

EXISTS BEYOND THE

HORIZON OF LOGIC

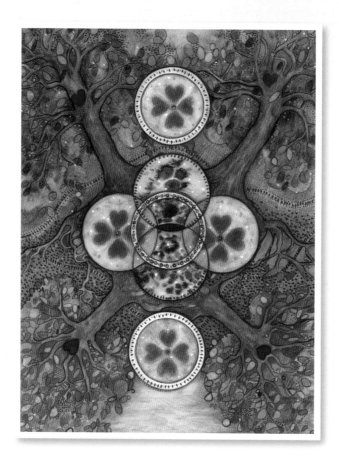

Love is an eternal light
Love is infinite

Love is the thread that binds
Every beautiful memory

Love is the *pulse of the Earth*
Love is the *rhythm of the stars*

Love is the moonlight that lovingly embraces the night
Love is a thought woven in silk
Love unfolds our destiny

THE GODDESS

lives eternally through you.

She is the invisible light that you feel in your heart.

She is the light that shines beyond the heavenly stars.

She is the eternal flame.

Through her we discover a

greater light.

She is a luminous shadow. She is a three-fold flame.

IN THE *hidden dimensions* OF YOUR SPIRIT, BEYOND THIS REALITY THERE ARE MANY OTHER REALITIES AND WORLDS, WORLDS WITHIN WORLDS THAT TRANSCEND TIME OR SPACE. ALL THAT IS, WAS, AND EVER WILL BE, IS PRESENT IN YOUR DNA. WHY SPEND OUR TIME WORRYING OR REMINISCING ABOUT THE PAST OR FUTURE, WHEN IT IS ALL HERE NOW INSIDE YOU? IF THE MIND IS ELSEWHERE YOU WILL MISS THE MAGIC BEING CREATED NOW. WHEN THE MIND DRIFTS TO THE PAST OR FUTURE IT IS NOT PRESENT.

ALL THINGS ARE BORN

IN AN *explosion of love*

THE *sacred flame* OF THE GODDESS
LIVES IN YOU
ALLOW HER FLAME TO GUIDE YOU
ALLOW IT TO LOVE YOU
AND IT WILL TRANSFORM YOU

When all hope seems lost,

you will discover a deeper truth.

A new beginning will emerge.

You will release all that you

have kept hidden.

You will step into the light.

You will see beyond the illusion

and you will realise that

only love is real.

Listen carefully

AND YOU WILL HEAR

YOUR INNER VOICE.

Look closely

AND YOU WILL SEE

THE LIGHT BEYOND

THE DARKNESS.

This moment I embrace you,

I HAVE LOVED YOU BEFORE THE DAWN OF TIME AND WILL CONTINUE

TO LOVE YOU, FOR THIS LOVE IS ETERNAL AND UNCHANGING. EVEN

AS OUR SOULS CHANGE THROUGH THE SEASONS OF ETERNITY,

THROUGH GREAT SPANS OF TIME, THROUGH ENDLESS AUTUMNS AND

WINTERS, SPRINGS AND SUMMERS, THROUGH ENDLESS SUNS AND

MOONS, THROUGH ENDLESS LOVES, JOYS AND SORROWS, THE LOVE

INSIDE US MAY DEEPEN BUT IT DOES NOT CHANGE, FOR THE ONE

GREAT LOVE STILL ILLUMINATES OUR HEARTS.

Eternity exists WITHIN YOUR HEART.

CLOSE YOUR EYES AND *feel your eternal presence.*

Nothing can exist without its opposite.

*Light and dark
exist in sacred union.*

Embrace your angels.
Embrace your demons.
Embrace all of who you are.

Love knows no separation –
it does not discriminate,
it does not judge,
it just is.

*Love and accept
yourself as you are.*

Drop the mask and just be you.

Beyond MY THOUGHTS

AND EARTHLY PERCEPTIONS

THERE EXISTS A WORLD

OF INFINITE CREATIVE POSSIBILITY,

A WORLD WHERE EVERYTHING

IS SPIRITUALLY CONNECTED.

THIS BEAUTIFUL PLANET

AND HER LOVING NATURE,

HER TREES, STREAMS,

MOUNTAINS AND SKY

ARE ALL A PART OF ME.

A UNIVERSE OF ENDLESS STARS,

THE SUN, THE MOON, EMBRACE ME

AND I LOVE THEM

JUST AS I LOVE YOU.

THERE IS A VISIBLE REALITY
AND AN INVISIBLE ONE

Both are equally real

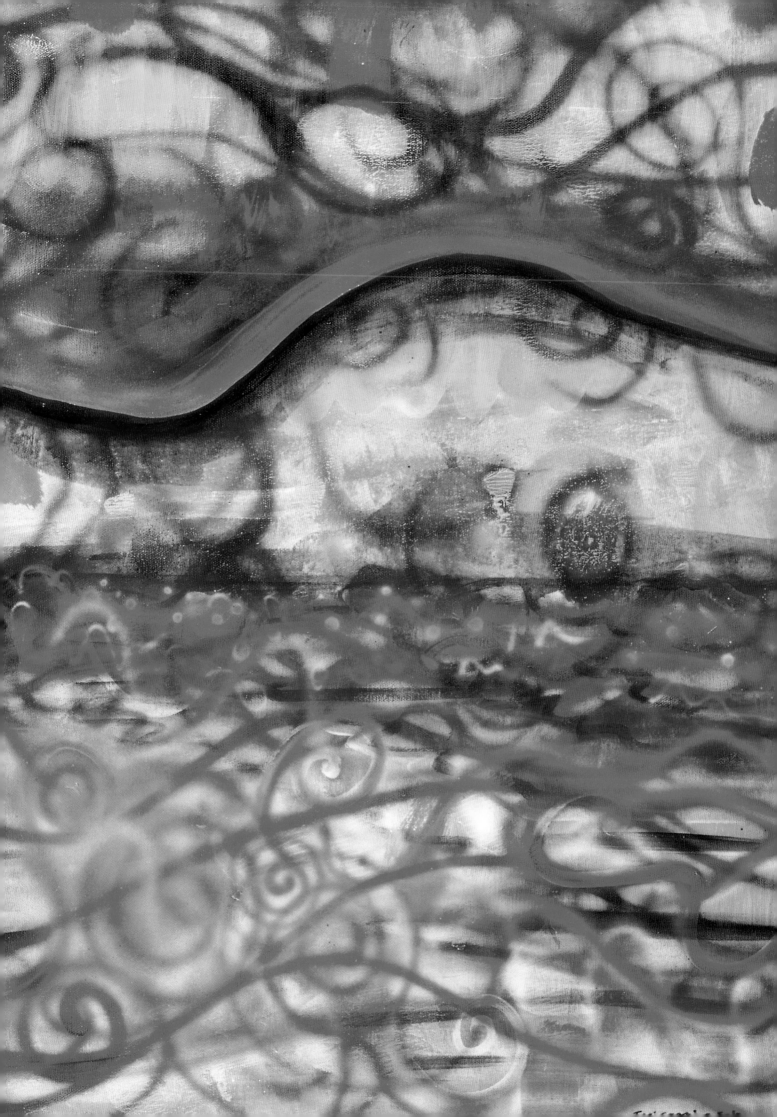

YOU ARE A *work of art*,
A MULTIDIMENSIONAL BEING
WITH NO BEGINNING OR END,
A FLOATING ISLAND
IN A COSMIC SEA OF LOVE.

UNFOLD YOUR DREAM;
BE EXTRAORDINARY,
FOR IN ESSENCE YOU ARE JUST THAT.

Follow
your heart

YOUR SACRED DUTY IS TO FOLLOW

the guidance of your soul

SO DO NOT LET FEAR CLOUD YOUR PURPOSE

YOUR *inner light* WILL SHOW YOU THE WAY

SHE IS YOUR WISDOM – TRUST IN HER

EVERY MOMENT IS PRECIOUS.   EVERY CHALLENGE A BLESSING.

EVERY DAY PRESENTS A NEW OPPORTUNITY

LOVE
FOREVER
UNFOLDS,
CREATES
AND
ILLUMINATES

LOVE
MOVES
THE
EARTH
AND
STARS

Create

For it is in creation that you exist

In this world full of wonder

Through love and hatred

Joy and sadness

Laughter and tears

The unknown awaits you

Step into the void

With courage and strength

Allow your inner light to unfold

Like a budding rose

Searching for the sun

Go where love leads you

Keep your pockets full of dreams

And allow them to be your guide

When you embrace the darkness

LIFE SEEMS BRIGHTER

All you need to know will be revealed
At the most perfect moment

It is pointless to resist life's natural flow.

Love is formless and timeless.
It has no boundaries,
apart from those we place upon it.
Love is limited only by our beliefs.

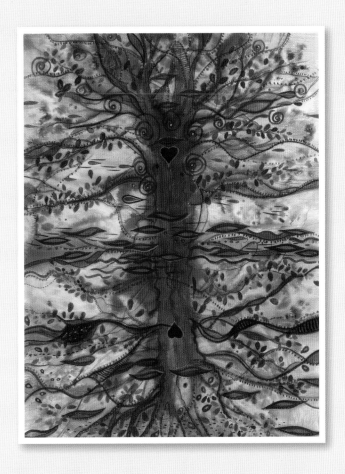

It is *human nature* to want to know

And to convert that knowing into a logical explanation.

However, true knowing is a matter only for the heart,

It cannot be explained or understood by a finite mind.

I suspect that I have a shadow and I suspect that my

shadow has been following me around.

I also suspect that it may be full of stuff, like -

shame, guilt, jealousy, anger?

Maybe even some feelings of inadequacy.

But in order to know for sure I must step out into

the light, only then will I know if I have a shadow,

only then can things be healed.

The rational mind

CANNOT GRASP THE CONCEPT THAT SOMETHING CAN EXIST
WITHOUT IT HAVING A BEGINNING AND AN ENDING.
IN OUR REALITY, THINGS ARE BORN AND THEN DIE,
THINGS BEGIN AND THEN END.
ON THE SURFACE THIS IS HOW LIFE APPEARS TO US.
HOWEVER WHEN WE DELVE DEEPER, INTO THE SUB-ATOMIC WORLD,
A DIFFERENT PICTURE EMERGES.
ENERGETICALLY, NOTHING ACTUALLY ENDS,
THINGS SIMPLY TRANSFORM.

Imagine a *golden path*

surrounded by lush trees and flowers.

The golden path is your life's journey,

the sun, your soul's guiding light.

Whether you know it or not

you are always on the right path.

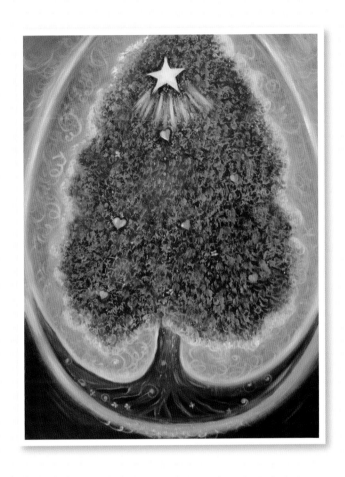

THE RATIONAL MIND CANNOT SENSE THE SPIRITUAL DIMENSIONS OF LIFE.
UNAWARE OF THE MULTIDIMENSIONAL REALITY OF SOUL
WHICH HAS NO BEGINNING OR END,
IT IS ONLY AWARE OF A SMALL PART OF WHAT ACTUALLY IS.
TO THE MIND EVERYTHING COMES TO AN END, SO ITS EQUATIONS,
ALL BASED ON IMPERMANENCE ARE THEREFORE FLAWED.

Life is always full of promise and potential.

You don't have to control or understand life;

you just need to allow it.

Endless creativity exists inside you;

a universe of light surrounds you.

A river of pure gold flows through you,

you are life yearning to experience ever greater love,

a beautiful unfolding story.

all you see is me
all you see is you
light always shines true
through the eternal light of love
forever aglow within each heart always

Great things are possible

WHEN EVERYTHING YOU DO

IS IN ALIGNMENT WITH YOUR

heartfelt vision AND PURPOSE

THE POWER

THAT MADE YOU

IS ULTIMATELY

THE POWER

THAT HEALS YOU

Trust your natural instincts.

No matter how professionally

something is presented,

if it doesn't feel right for you,

then it's not.

Beyond THE HORIZON
OF SPACE AND TIME,
THERE IS A WORLD OF DREAMS,
A WORLD WITHOUT LIMITS,
FULL OF MAGICAL IDEAS,
A WORLD JUST WAITING
FOR YOU TO ENTER.
AND YET THIS MAGICAL WORLD
IS NOT FAR AWAY
FOR IT EXISTS INSIDE YOU –
AND A DREAM IS ALL IT TAKES
TO GET THERE.

Every time you see *beauty* in another,

Let it serve to remind you of your own beauty.

The stream that flows through you

flows through all creation.

And yet, what flows from your stream

is always unique to you.

Feel the grass alive
and moving. Feel the
trees breathing. All is
alight with love. Feel
a deep peace
settle within
you.

Toni Carmine Salerno

There is nothing more important
than this present moment.
Be still.
Feel a gentle breeze blow.

Beyond the breeze you can feel
a place beyond time;
a state of peace beyond your thoughts.
Light transforming to ever-greater love.

An eternal glow
that always was and always will be.

I am one with the universe,
one with the eternal Goddess,
who is a part of me.

My heart is filled
with her infinite wisdom and love.
She is the endless stream of creativity
that flows through me.

Through you

I see the hidden parts

of myself.

I feel the soul

of the Earth.

I intuitively know

the secret meaning

of the stars.

In you,

I see my own reflection.

My soul is an ocean
forever longing for your shore.

You are the thought that
ebbs and flows within my dreams.

My eternal flame.

Gently close your eyes and as you quiet your mind,
relax every muscle and joint.
Let go of all tension and
bring your focus to your breath.
Imagine yourself breathing in light.
As you breathe out,
breathe out all unwanted thoughts.
Feel a gentle breeze flow through your mind –
feel it clear away any concerns or negative feelings.

...Breathe in light...

...Breathe out love...

The *old structures* are crumbling both within and around us.

Much of what we believed to be true is no longer true for us.

We are searching for deeper truths; we are searching for soul,

our own soul and the soul of the earth.

For like us the earth does have a soul, a very beautiful one.

She, Gaia, the Earth Mother and Goddess is a living jewel,

our beautiful blue planet is in transition

and as we let go of the past a new future is being born.

Celebration is a ritual

through which we *honour our blessings.*

Before embarking on the next step,

stop and celebrate what you already have.

WITHIN

the heart of the Goddess

GOD RESTS AND DREAMS

She is the miracle

and magic of life

SHE COMES TO HELP YOU FULFIL YOUR DREAMS

IN THE PURPLE OF NIGHT

THE SILENCE IS SHATTERED

A new day is born

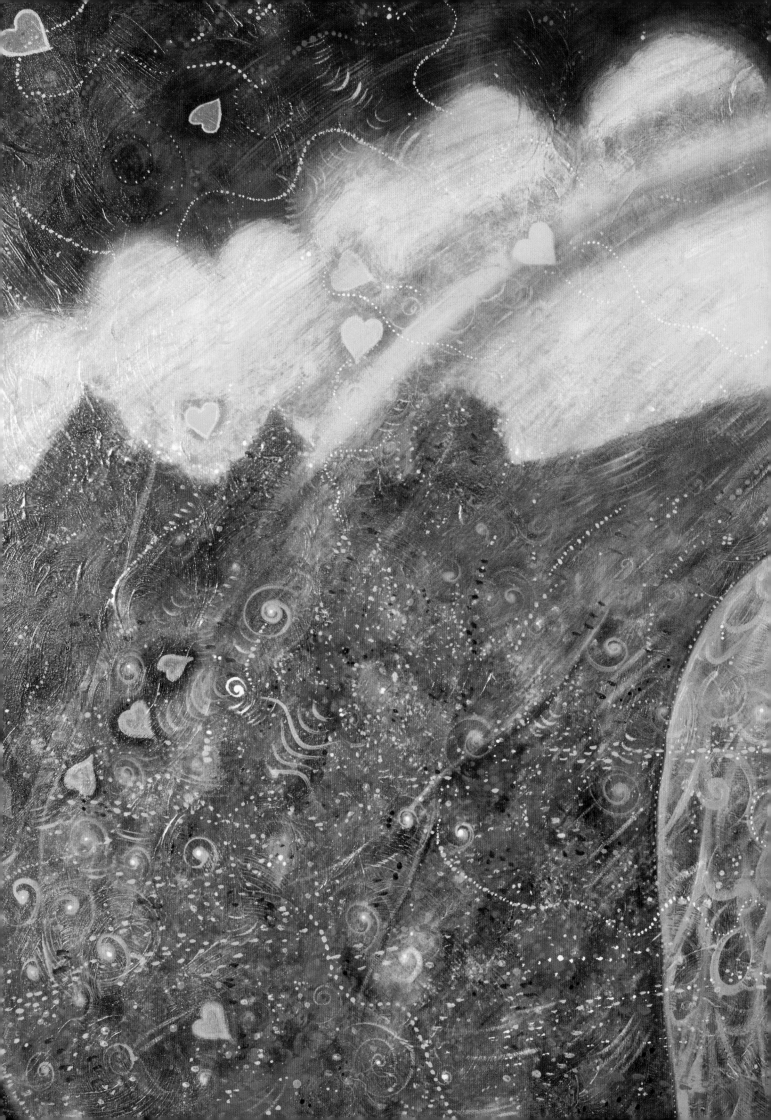

She dreamt you into being,
like a whirlwind from heaven you appeared,
just as she appears and reappears
through her endless forms and manifestations,
for she is in essence you,
she is in essence the ocean
and every tree and leaf of grass.

In your heart
you will find
the missing
pieces

You awoke in me a deep and profound love.

I remember a glance from afar, in a past life.

It made an impression on my heart.

You gave me wings as I wept.

Silently, as the world turns my words into a memory,

I want to tell you that you gave my life meaning,

I want to tell you that I love you.

About the Author & Artist

TONI CARMINE SALERNO is an internationally recognised bestselling author and artist. Through his work which transcends cultures and borders, he explores universal and timeless themes such as spirituality, poetry, philosophy and love. His paintings are collected by people from around the globe and his publications are available in over 15 languages.

Toni's work is infused with a soulful healing energy that helps us to connect to our spiritual selves; they are meditations in paint and colour that guide us to an infinite source of love and wisdom that we each hold within. His work continues to quietly illuminate hearts and minds around the globe.

For more information on Toni's work, please visit the following websites:
www.tonicarminesalerno.com
www.blueangelonline.com